My ABC's

J Merrill Publishing, Inc.
434 Hillpine Drive
Columbus, OH 43207
www.JMerrill.pub

Library of Congress Control Number: 2022906810
ISBN-13: 978-1-954414-46-4 (Paperback)
ISBN-13: 978-1-954414-45-7 (eBook)

Book Title: My ABC's
Author: Christy Grogg

My ABC's

Dedicated to my children

"Always Be Who You Are"

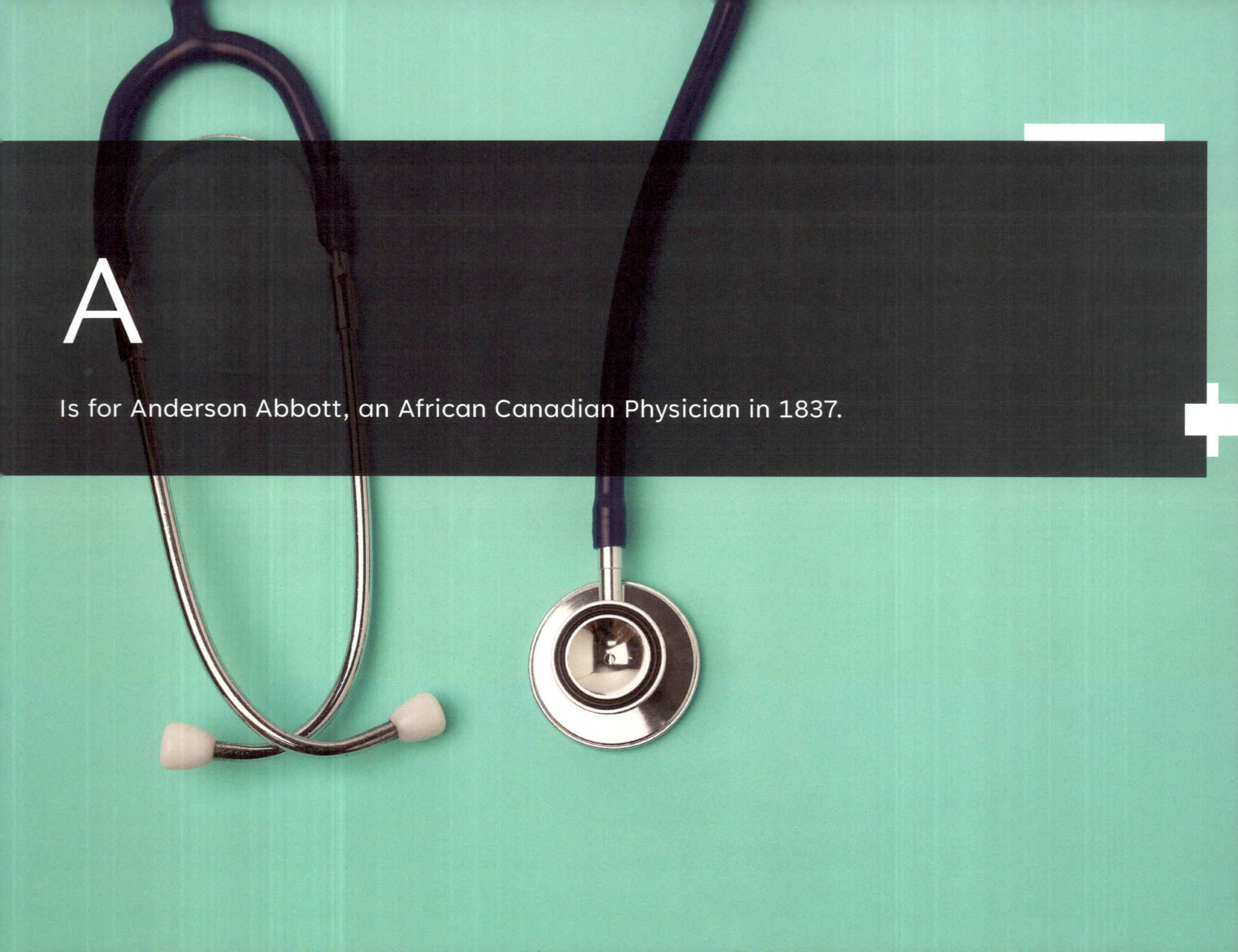

A

Is for Anderson Abbott, an African Canadian Physician in 1837.

B

Is for Booker T. Washington, the founder of the Tuskegee Normal and Industrial Institute.

C

Is for Condoleezza Rice, the first Black female US Secretary of State.

D

Is for Denmark Vesey, the first enslaved carpenter who purchased his freedom in 1822.

E

Is for Ella Fitzgerald, a famous jazz singer.

F

Is for Frederick Douglass; he launched the abolitionist newspaper in 1846.

G

Is for George Washington Carver; he testified at the congressional tariff hearing in 1921. He was also known as the Peanut Man.

H

Is for Harriet Tubman. In 1849, she helped slaves escape from slavery.

I

Is for Ira Aldridge, a famous
black theater actor.

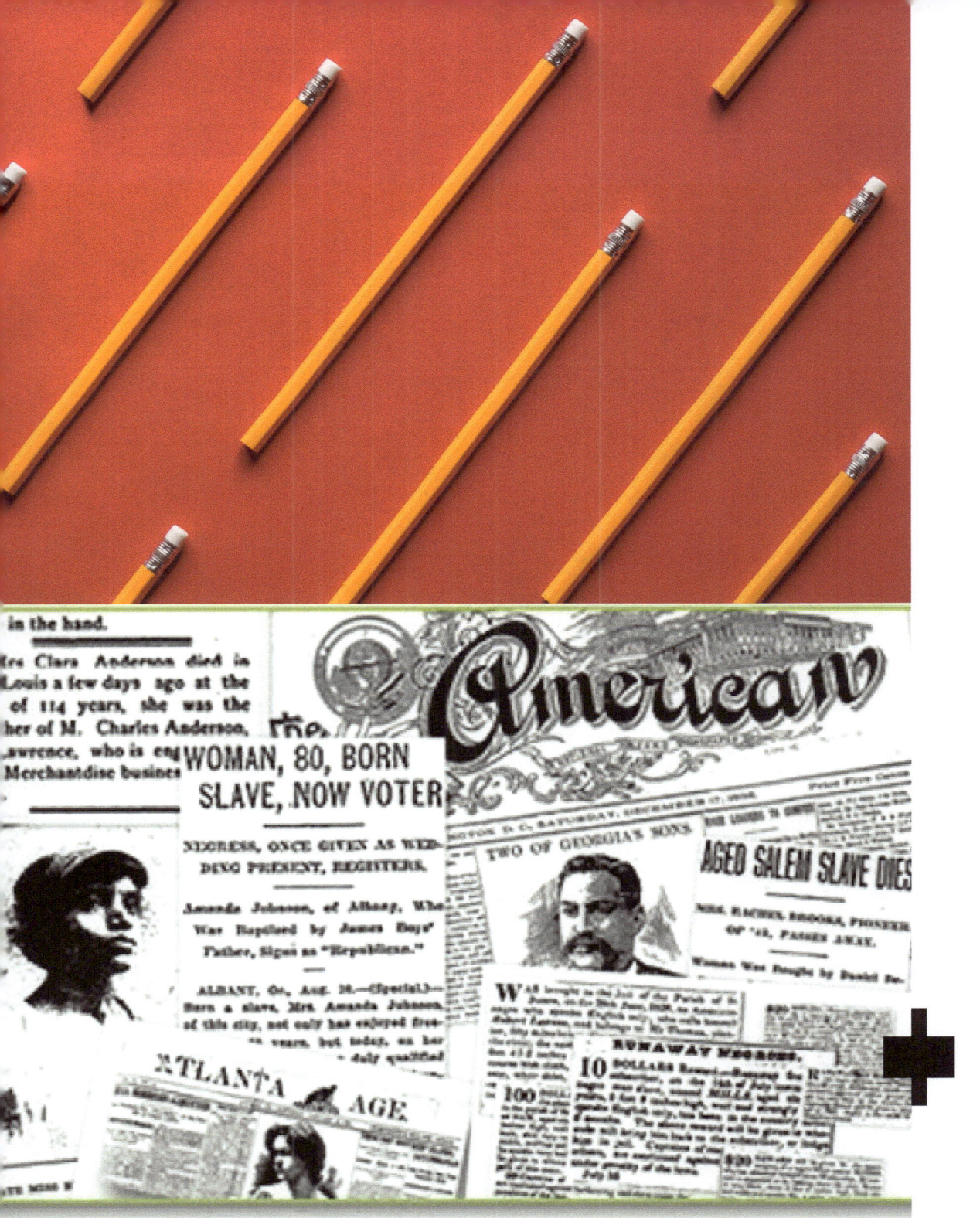

J

Is for Joel Rogers, a journalist for the Black Press in 1934.

K

Is for Kathleen Battle, a black opera singer.

L

Is for Lewis Lattimore, who invented the electric lamp. He was also the only African American involved in the Thomas Edison Laboratory.

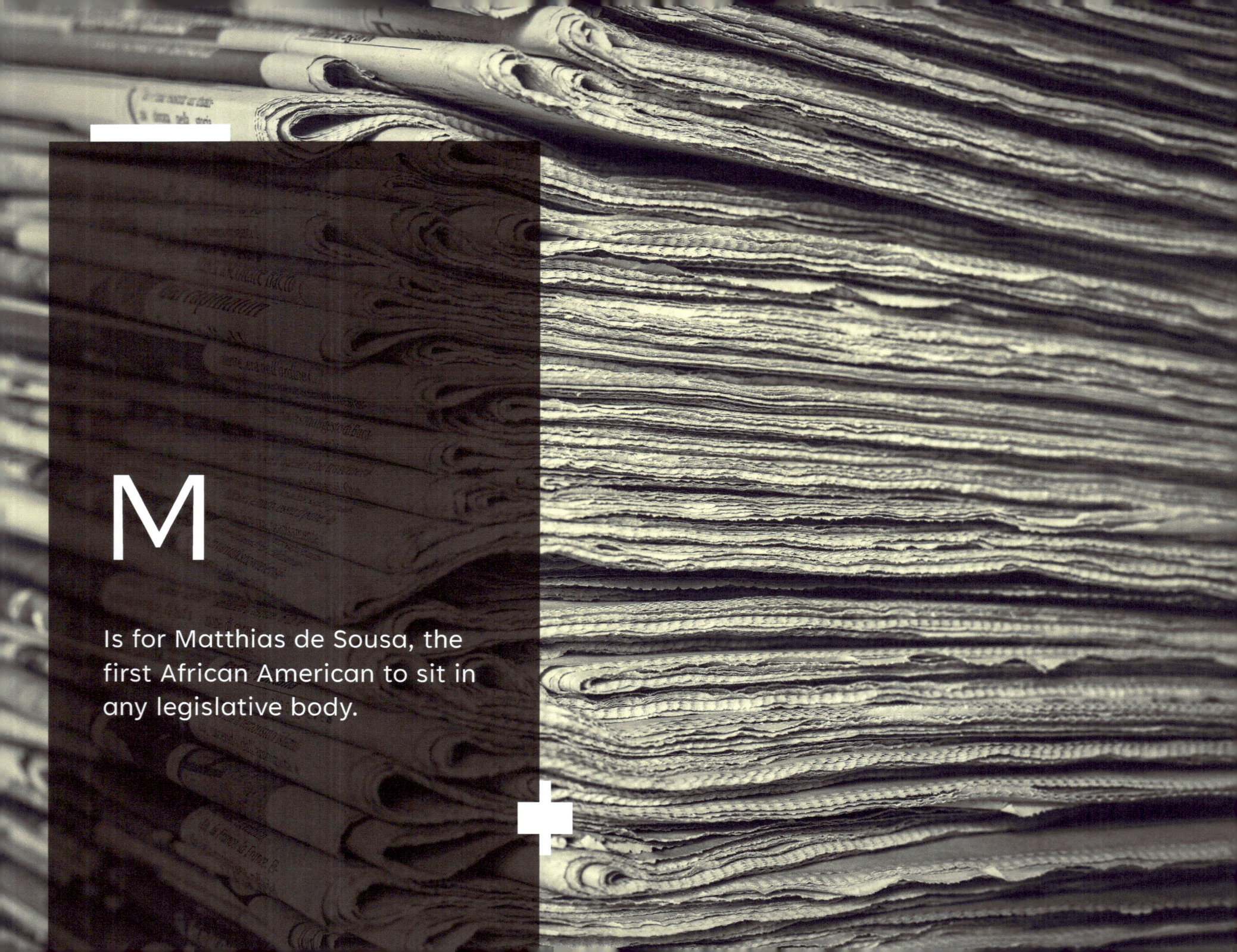

M

Is for Matthias de Sousa, the first African American to sit in any legislative body.

N

Is for Nathaniel Cole, the First African American Television Show Host in 1956.

O

Is for Ossie Davis, a famous actor, and writer.

P

Is a Paul Robeson; he was the 3rd African American to earn a scholarship from Rutgers University.

Q

Is for Quincy Troupe, a professional baseball player, and amateur boxing champion.

R

Is for Ralph Ellison; he was the managing editor for the Negro Quarterly in New York.

S

Is for Sojourner Truth, an abolitionist and women's rights activist.

T

Is for Theo Allain, who was a famous black farmer.

U

Is for Ulysses Dearing; he was the first African American to own a major restaurant in Cleveland, Ohio.

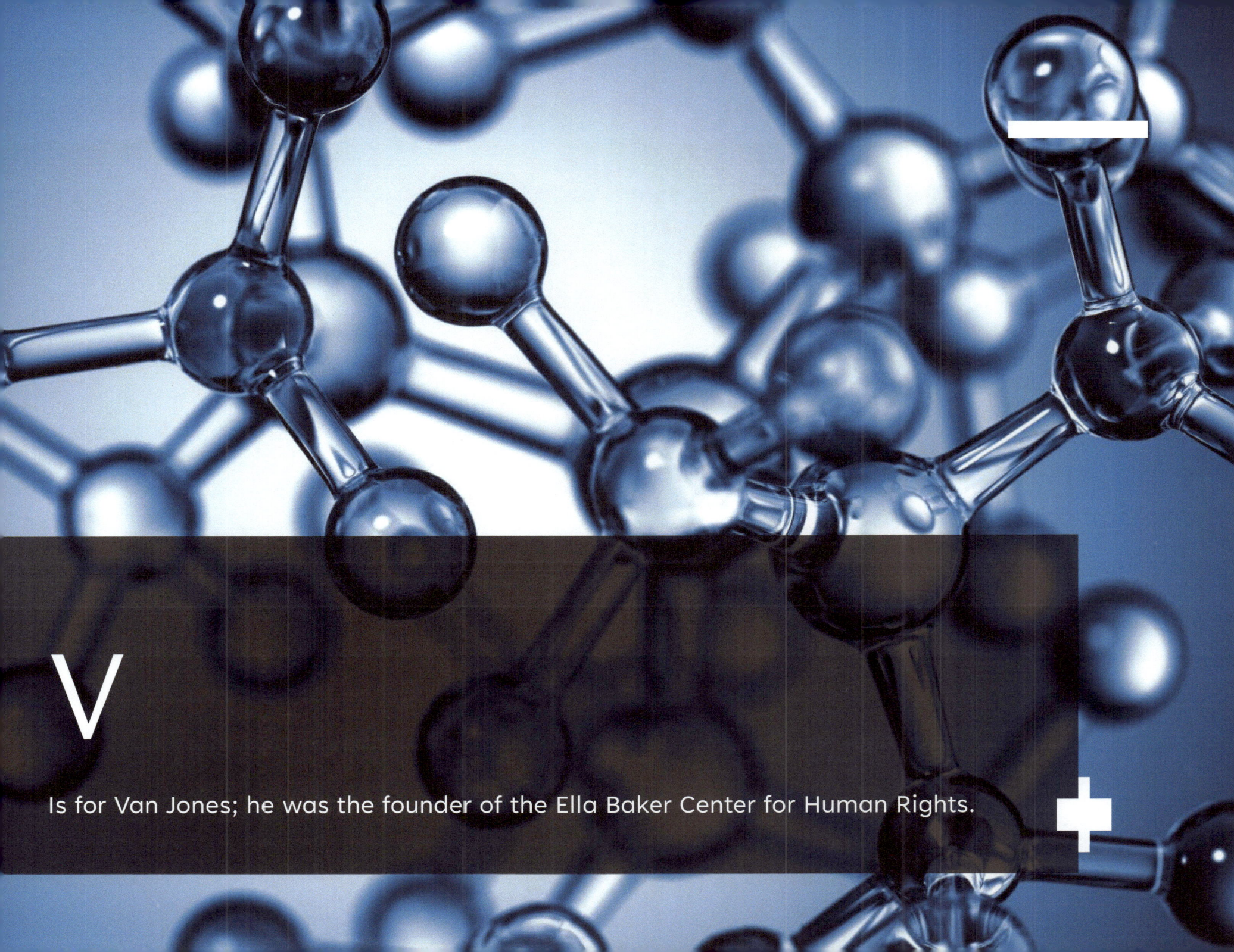

V

Is for Van Jones; he was the founder of the Ella Baker Center for Human Rights.

W

Is for Will Allen; he was an urban Farmer that turned his production into the delivery of meals.

X

Is for Xavier Thomas, a famous football player.

Y

Is for York, an African male that helped lead the Lewis and Clark Expedition. He was the first African American to see the Pacific Ocean.

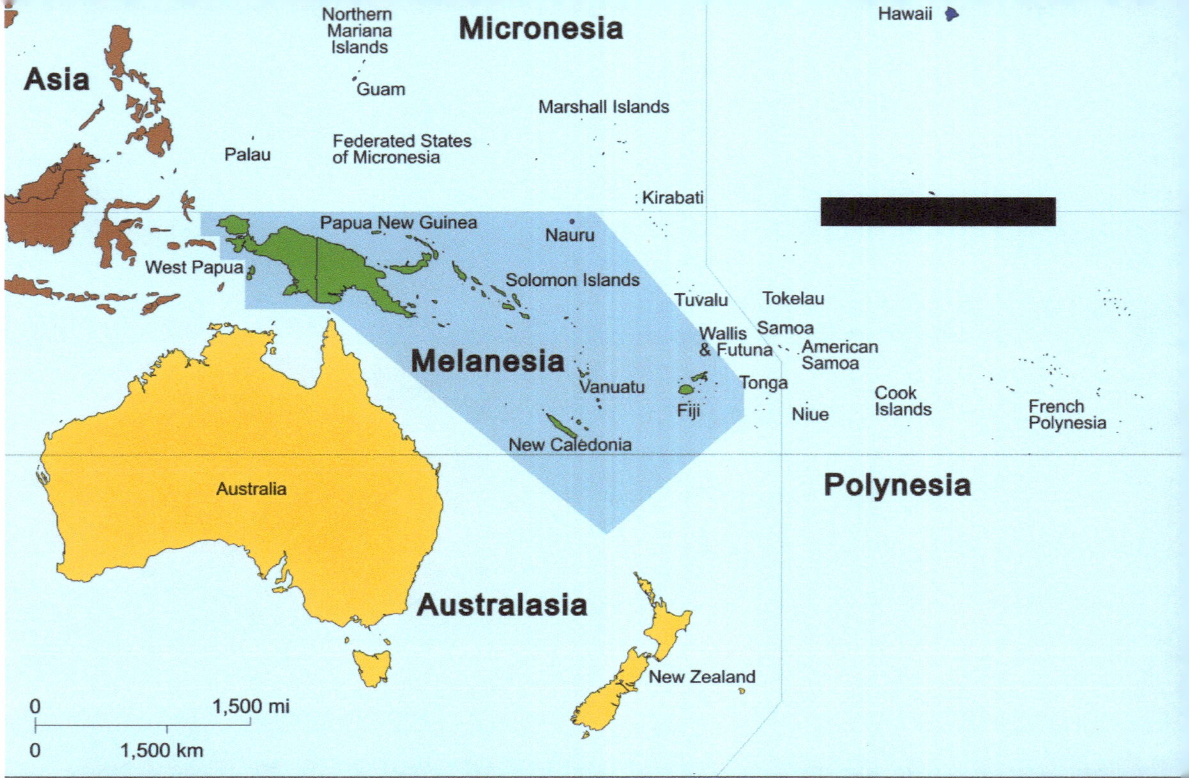

Z

Is for Zora Neale Hurston;
she was considered one of
the most preeminent
writers of the 20th century.

About the Author

Christy Grogg is a single mother of four children and eleven grandchildren. She is considered a jack of all trades. She has a bachelor's in psychology. She currently lives in a small town in Ohio, where she still strives to teach her grandchildren about Black History.

www.ingramcontent.com/pod-product-compliance
Lightning Source LLC
Chambersburg PA
CBHW040819120626

46551CB00004B/602